Johnny

Story by Leslie Falconer
Pictures by Chris Lensch

First published by Experience Early Learning Co.
7243 Scotchwood Lane, Grawn, Michigan 49637 USA

ISBN: 978-1-937954-27-6
Visit us at www.ExperienceEarlyLearning.com

Johnny loved apples.

He ate apples for breakfast.

He ate apples for lunch.

He ate apples for dinner.

But he always ate alone. This made Johnny sad.

So, Johnny decided to share his apples with others.

First, he walked to Ohio.

Ohio

The path to Ohio
twisted and turned!

Along the way a few
seeds tumbled
out of his pouch.

When he arrived in Ohio,
he planted two seeds.
The two seeds grew into
two trees that produced
many apples.

People were excited
to see the apples.
They picked them
and took them home.

Together, they ate apples for breakfast. They ate apples for lunch. They ate apples for dinner.

Johnny liked making friends,
so he decided to share his apples
with others.

Next, he walked to Michigan.

Michigan

The path to Michigan was bumpy!

bounced

Along the way some seeds out of his pouch.

When he arrived in Michigan
Johnny planted four seeds.

The four seeds grew
into four trees that
produced many apples.

The townsfolk
were amazed!

16

They picked the apples and
took them home.

Together, they ate apples for breakfast. They ate apples for lunch. They ate apples for dinner.

Johnny decided to share his apples with even more people.

Finally, he walked to Indiana.

Indiana

The path to Indiana was windy!
Along the way some seeds blew
out of his pouch.

When Johnny arrived in Indiana, he decided to plant his last six seeds, but all of the seeds were gone!

OH, NO!

Without the seeds, he could not share the gift of apple trees with anyone else.

But then Johnny noticed a small
brown squirrel. He was holding
something in his paws.

The missing apple seeds!

The squirrel shared the seeds with Johnny. Together they planted six seeds. The seeds grew into six trees that produced many apples.

People were excited to see the apples. They picked them and took them home.

They all ate apples for breakfast.

They all ate apples
for lunch.

They all ate apples
for dinner.

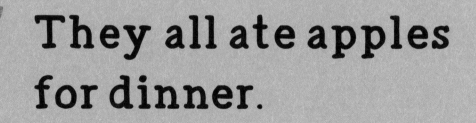

The End

The Real Johnny Appleseed

Johnny Appleseed's real name was John Chapman.

He was a vegetarian.

He used some of his income to purchase mistreated horses so he could place them in safe and healthy environments.

He was very wealthy, although he did not flaunt his wealth.

He didn't just plant apple seeds. He also carried the seeds for medicinal plants, as well as the plants themselves.

He was a Christian missionary.